Anna Myers

Ninja Air Fryer
Cookbook UK
for Beginners

Easy and Crispy Home Made Meals for Your Ninja Air Fryer Max to Bake, Fry and Toast

All rights reserved

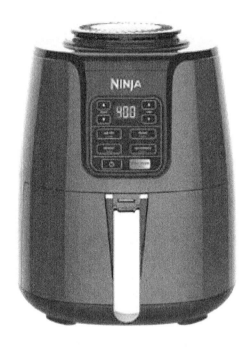

ISBN : 9798378789528

Content

Introduction **6**

1. Fish finger sandwiches 7
2. Bacon and Pepper breakfast hash 8
3. N'Duja aubergine Parmigiana 9
4. Cauliflower buffalo bites with ranch dressing 10
5. Salt and pepper chilli chips 11
6. Dijon-crusted salmon 12
7. Herbed lemon chicken and vegetables 13
8. Pork loin with vegetables 14
9. Chicken Wings 15
10. Chicken Breast 16
11. Asparagus 17
12. Crispy Potato Chips 18
13. Baked Potato 19
14. Brussels Sprouts 20
15. Potato Wedges 21
16. Fried Tofu 22
17. Healthy Salmon 23
18. Buffalo Cauliflower Bites 24
19. Healthy Eggplant 25
20. Quick Broccoli 26
21. Blooming onion (vegan) 27
22. Corn on the cob 28
23. Frozen Tater Tots 29
24. Zucchini Chips 30

25. Air Fryer Okra 31

26. Homemade pizza rolls 32

27. Hard boiled eggs 33

28. Mozzarella Sticks 34

29. Crispy Frozen French Fries Without Oil 35

30. Sweet Potato Fries 36

31. Air Fried Bacon 37

32. Air fried steak 38

33. Air fryer shrimp 39

34. Meatloaf 40

35. Burritos 41

36. Hamburgers 42

37. Crispy Air Fried Fish 43

38. Onion Rings 44

39. Crispy tortilla chips 45

40. Quick and Easy Meatballs 46

41. Tilapia without Breading 47

42. Zucchini Chips 48

43. Garlic Parmesan Carrot Fries 49

44. Roasted Potatoes 50

45. Stuffed peppers 51

46. Crispy Tofu 52

47. Nachos 53

48. Crispy Eggplant Parmesan 54

49. Chicken Nuggets 55

50. Apple Chips 56

51. Crispy Air Fryer Chicken Wings 57

52. Air Fryer Falafel 58

53. Air Fryer Chicken Tenders 59

54. Air Fryer Sweet Potato Fries 60

55.   Air Fryer Salmon 61

56.   Air Fryer Pork Chops 62

57.   Air Fryer Vegetable Spring Rolls 63

58.   Air Fryer Parmesan Crusted Chicken 64

59.   Air Fryer Baked Potatoes 65

60.   Air Fryer Coconut Shrimp 66

61.   Air Fryer Meatballs 67

62.   Air Fryer Zucchini Fries 68

63.   Air Fryer Mozzarella Sticks 69

64.   Air Fryer Teriyaki Chicken 70

65.   Air Fryer Onion Rings 71

66.   Air Fryer BBQ Ribs 72

67.   Air Fryer Stuffed Mushrooms 73

68.   Air Fryer Fried Chicken 74

69.   Air Fryer Garlic Bread 75

70.   Air Fryer Cinnamon Sugar Donuts 76

71.   Air Fryer Beef Skewers 77

72.   Air Fryer Buffalo Cauliflower 78

73.   Air Fryer Caramelized Bananas 79

74.   Air Fryer Bacon 80

75.   Air Fryer Pork Rinds 81

76.   Air Fryer Tofu 82

77.   Air Fryer Fried Shrimp 83

78.   Air Fryer Chimichangas 84

79.   Air Fryer Apple Chips 85

80.   Air Fryer Pesto Chicken 86

Introduction

The Ninja Air Fryer is a versatile kitchen appliance that allows you to cook a wide range of delicious, crispy foods with minimal oil. It is a relatively new product in the market and has become increasingly popular due to its unique features and functionalities. The appliance has been designed with the latest technology to help you achieve perfect results every time.

One of the key features of the Ninja Air Fryer is its wide temperature range, which allows you to cook at temperatures ranging from 40°C to 220°C. This makes it easy to cook a wide range of recipes, including meats, vegetables, and even desserts. The air fryer also has a range of pre-set functions, including Air Fry, Roast, Reheat, Dehydrate, and Max Crisp, which help to simplify the cooking process.

The Ninja Air Fryer uses a combination of high-speed air circulation and a powerful fan to circulate hot air around the food, cooking it evenly and giving it a crispy texture. This means you can enjoy your favorite fried foods with up to 75% less fat than traditional frying methods, making it a healthier alternative.

The appliance is also equipped with a large-capacity basket that can hold up to 5.2 liters of food, making it ideal for cooking for larger families or groups of friends. The basket is non-stick and dishwasher safe, making it easy to clean and maintain.

In addition to its air frying capabilities, the Ninja Air Fryer can also be used for baking, roasting, and dehydrating food. This makes it a versatile and multi-functional kitchen appliance that can be used for a wide range of cooking applications.

Overall, the Ninja Air Fryer is a must-have kitchen appliance for anyone who loves to cook and enjoys crispy, delicious food. Its unique features, ease of use, and healthy cooking benefits make it a great addition to any kitchen.

Fish finger sandwiches

Servings: 4

Ingredients

- 75g golden crumbs
- 50g (15) Ritz Crackers, crushed
- 50g flour
- 500g uncooked cod, cut into finger sizes (2.5cm by 10cm)
- Cooking Spray
- 2 teaspoons Dijon mustard
- 2 eggs, whisked
- Flaked sea salt
- pepper to taste
- 8 slices white bread
- Tartar sauce or ketchup
- Iceburg lettuce, shredded

Preparation

1. Place mustard, eggs and salt to taste in a shallow bowl, whisk together. Place crumbs and cracker crumbs in another shallow dish. Dip each finger in flour, dip each fish finger in mustard egg mixture, then dredge in breadcrumbs and continue until breaded.
2. Insert the crisper plate into the basket and the basket into the appliance. Preheat the appliance by selecting AIR FRY, setting the temperature to 180°C and setting the time to 3 minutes. Press START/STOP to begin.
3. Select AIR FRY, set the temperature to 180°C and set the time to 8 minutes. Select START/STOP to begin.
4. After 4 minutes, flip the fish, spray the other side and reinsert the basket to resume cooking. Repeat until all the fish sticks are cooked.
5. Spread tartar sauce or ketchup on a slice of bread, add lettuce and 3 fish sticks for each sandwich.

Bacon and Pepper breakfast hash

Servings: 4

Ingredients

- 2 white potatoes, peeled, diced
- 1 teaspoon paprika
- 1 teaspoon ground black pepper, plus more for seasoning
- 1 teaspoon celery or garlic salt
- 225g uncooked streaky bacon, cut in 1cm pieces
- 1 small onion, peeled, diced
- 1 red bell pepper, diced
- 1 teaspoon sea salt, plus more for seasoning
- 4 eggs

Preparation

1. Remove the vegetable tray from the dish and insert the dish into the appliance.
2. Preheat the appliance by selecting ROAST, setting the temperature to 180°C and setting the time to 3 minutes. Select START/STOP to begin.
3. After 3 minutes, add the bacon to the skillet. Reinsert the pan. Select ROAST, set the temperature to 180°C and set the time to 45 minutes.
4. Select START/STOP to begin. Cook for 5 minutes or until bacon is crisp, stirring occasionally.
5. After 5 minutes, remove the pan from the device and add the onion, pepper, potatoes and spices. Stir to incorporate. Reinsert the pan to resume cooking.
6. Cook for 35 minutes, stirring occasionally, until the potatoes are cooked through and golden brown.
7. Once the vegetables are browned, remove the pan from the device and crack four eggs on the surface of the mince.
8. Season with additional salt and pepper to taste. Reinsert the pan to resume cooking.
9. Cook 3 to 5 minutes or until eggs are cooked to your preference.
10. Serve immediately.

N'Duja aubergine Parmigiana

Servings: 4

Ingredients

For the sauce:
- 1 tin plum tomatoes
- 1 lemon (zested)
- Large handful fresh basil
- 2 shallots - finely diced
- 25g N'duja
- Pinch sea salt
- Olive oil

For the aubergine:
- 2 Eggs - beaten
- 200g Panko breadcrumbs
- 300g Burrata (Drained/patted dry)
- 8 Large basil leaves
- 2 large aubergines
- 200g Plain flour
- Pinch of seasoning: salt, pepper, smoked paprika
- 200g Parmesan cheese

Preparation

1. Slice eggplant into 1-inch-thick rounds and place on a baking rack
2. Season with salt and set aside
3. In a frying pan, heat a few tablespoons of olive oil, add the chopped shallots and cook for a few minutes until soft.
4. Add the n'duja and cook for a minute
5. Add the Italian tomatoes and mash them with a fork as you go into the pan
6. Add the basil, lemon zest and the juice of half the lemon
7. Reduce for 5-10 minutes until thickened and saucy. Season to taste and set aside
8. In another bowl, season the flour with salt, pepper and paprika
9. Lay out three dishes and transfer the seasoned flour, beaten eggs and panko breadcrumbs to each. Individually coat the eggplant slices with flour, egg and finally breadcrumbs
10. Transfer the coated eggplant in a single layer to the Ninja Air Fryer and cook on the "Crisp" setting at 200 degrees for five minutes
11. While cooking, slice the burrata
12. Layer the cooked eggplant, basil leaf, sauce and burrata several times to create three layers. Cover the top layer with grated parmesan and return to the air fryer to cook for another eight minutes on the crispy setting

Cauliflower buffalo bites with ranch dressing

Servings: 4

Ingredients

Ingredients:
- 1 tsp ground cumin
- 1 tsp paprika
- salt, as desired
- ground black pepper, as desired
- 250ml unsweetened plant-based milk
- 700g cauliflower, cut into 5cm florets
- cooking spray
- 150g gram flour
- 1 tsp onion powder
- 1 tsp garlic powder
- 30ml sunflower oil
- 70ml buffalo sauce

Ranch Dressing:
- 50ml unsweetened plant-based milk
- 1 tbsp fresh chopped parsley
- 1 tbsp fresh chopped chives
- 100ml egg free mayonnaise
- 1 tsp garlic powder
- 1 tsp onion powder

Preparation

1. In a large bowl, add the gram flour, onion powder, garlic powder, cumin, paprika, salt and pepper. Add the milk little by little until you obtain a smooth paste.
2. Dip the cauliflower florets in the batter to coat them evenly.
3. Insert the crisper plates into the two zone drawers, then spray the crisper plate with oil. Arrange the cauliflower in an even layer in both drawers.
4. Select zone 1, turn the dial to select AIR FRY, set the temperature to 170c and set the time to 15 minutes. Select MATCH. Press the knob to start cooking.
5. While the cauliflower cooks, prepare the buffalo sauce. In a small bowl, whisk the oil and buffalo sauce together.
6. Reinsert the baskets into the unit. Select zone 1, turn the dial to select AIR FRY, set the temperature to 170c and set the time to 12 minutes. Select MATCH. Press the knob to start cooking.
7. While the cauliflower cooks, prepare the ranch dressing. In a small bowl, combine all dressing ingredients until smooth.
8. When done cooking, serve Buffalo Cauliflower Bites with ranch dressing.

Salt and pepper chili chips

Ingredients

- 1-2 red chillis, sliced
- 1 garlic clove crushed
- 2 spring onion, sliced into 2cm strips
- 600g potatoes, cut into chips about 1cm thickness
- 1/2 red pepper thinly sliced
- 1/2 white onion thinly sliced
- 1 tbsp cooking oil

Seasoning:
- 1 tsp white pepper
- 1 tsp Chinese 5 spice
- 1 tsp fine salt
- 1/4 tsp chili powder
- 1/4 tsp msg(optional) if using cut the salt to 1/2 tsp

Preparation

1. Soak your fries in water for at least 30 minutes, drain and pat dry. Season with salt and pepper
2. drizzle with oil, mixing well. Bake in your Air-fryer for 20 minutes at 200°C until golden and crispy.
3. Meanwhile, heat a wok or sauté pan and brown the white onions for 1 minute, then add the
4. peppers, fry for another minute and add spring onions and garlic.
5. Add the fries and toss the wok to combine well, season with the salt and pepper seasoning and toss everything together
6. again.
7. Serve as a side dish with your favorite fakeaway.

Dijon-crusted salmon

Servings: 4

Ingredients

- 1/4 tsp ground black pepper, plus more to taste
- 2 tbsp Dijon mustard, divided
- 4 uncooked skinless salmon fillets
- 50g panko bread crumbs
- 2 tbsp fresh parsley, chopped
- 1 tbsp olive oil
- 1/4 tsp sea salt, plus more to taste
- (170g each)
- NADA Lemon wedges, for serving

Preparation

1. Grease the vegetable tray. Insert the greased vegetable tray into the pan and the pan into the unit. Preheat the appliance by
2. selecting ROAST, setting the temperature to 170°C and setting the time to 5 minutes. Select START/STOP to begin.
3. In a bowl, mix the breadcrumbs, parsley, olive oil, salt and pepper until well blended. Put aside.
4. Spread 1/2 tablespoon of Dijon mustard on all sides of each salmon fillet. Season the fillets with salt and pepper, then coat each fillet evenly with the breadcrumb mixture.
5. Once the unit is preheated, place the coated fillets on the crisper plate. Select ROAST, set the temperature to 170°C and set the time to 20 minutes. Select START/STOP to begin.
6. Cooking is complete when the internal temperature reaches 65°C and the breadcrumbs are golden brown. At the end of cooking, serve the fillets with a squeeze of lemon.

Herbed lemon chicken and vegetables

Servings: 4

Ingredients

- 2 tsp fresh thyme, chopped, divided
- 3/4 tsp sea salt, divided
- 1 tsp ground black pepper
- 3 tbsp lemon juice
- 1 tsp fresh rosemary, chopped
- 2 golden potatoes, peeled, diced
- 1 large carrot, peeled, diced
- 1 onion, peeled, thinly sliced
- 3 tbsp olive oil, divided
- 2 tsp lemon zest, divided
- 2 uncooked boneless skinless
- NADA chicken breasts (225g each)

Preparation

1. In a large bowl, combine potatoes, carrot, onion, 1 tbsp oil, 1 tsp lemon zest, 1 tsp thyme, 1/4 tsp salt and ½ teaspoon of pepper. Stir to combine.
2. Place remaining ingredients, except chicken, in shallow bowl. Stir to combine. Add the chicken breasts and toss to coat.
3. Insert the crisper plate into the dish and the dish into the device. Preheat the appliance by selecting ROAST, setting the temperature to 170°C and setting the time to 5 minutes. Select START/STOP to begin.
4. After 5 minutes, place the vegetable mixture on a vegetable sheet in a single layer. Place the chicken breasts over the vegetables. Reinsert the pan.
5. Select ROAST, set the temperature to 170°C and set the time to 35 minutes. Select START/STOP to begin.
6. After 20 minutes, remove the mold. Remove the chicken and mix the vegetables. Return chicken to skillet, turning to cook evenly. Reinsert the pan to resume cooking.
7. Cooking is complete when the internal temperature of the chicken reaches 75°C. Once cooked, serve the chicken with roasted vegetables.

Pork loin with vegetables

Servings: 4

Ingredients

- 3 tsp sea salt, divided
- 3 tsp ground black pepper, divided
- 2 tsp fresh oregano, chopped
- 1 medium courgette, cut in 2.5cm pieces
- 1 yellow pepper, cut in 2.5cm pieces
- 1 red onion, peeled, cut in eighths
- 1 tbsp olive oil
- 1 uncooked pork loin roast (750g)

Preparation

1. In a large mixing bowl, toss the zucchini, bell pepper and onion (making sure to separate the onion layers) with 1 tsp salt, 1 tsp pepper, oregano and oil of olives. Season the pork loin on all sides with the remaining salt and pepper.
2. Insert the crisper plate into the dish and the dish into the device. Preheat the appliance by selecting AIR FRY, setting the temperature to 160°C and setting the time to 3 minutes. Select START/STOP to begin.
3. After 3 minutes, place the vegetables on the crusty plate. Place pork, fat side down, over vegetables; reinsert the pan.
4. Select AIR FRY, set the temperature to 160°C and set the time to 50 minutes. Select START/STOP to begin.
5. After 20 minutes, remove the skillet from the appliance and turn the pork over. Reinsert the pan to resume cooking.
6. Cooking is complete when the internal temperature reaches 65°C. Remove the skillet and allow the pork to cool for 5-10 minutes before serving.

Chicken Wings

Servings: 4

Ingredients

- 1 teaspoon garlic powder
- 1 tsp onion powder
- 1 teaspoon paprika
- 1 kg chicken wings (drums and flats) (defrosted if frozen)
- 1 TBS olive oil
- 1 teaspoon salt
- ½ tsp black pepper

Preparation

1. Prepare the chicken wings. If the wings are full, separate them into drums and flats. Make sure they are thawed. Dry them completely (this will help them become crispy).

2. Place the wings in a bowl and drizzle them with olive oil. Mix to coat. Add garlic powder, onion powder, paprika, salt and pepper. Toss to coat the wings well.

3. Preheat the Air Fryer to 160°C for 2 minutes. Add the wings in a single layer to the air fryer (they should NOT be touching) and cook for 10 minutes at 400 degrees F.

4. Once the timer is off, carefully open and flip the chicken wings. Cook another 8 minutes. Remove the chicken wings and serve.

Chicken Breast

Ingredients

- 2 teaspoons olive oil
- 1 teaspoon paprika
- ½ teaspoon garlic powder
- 2 boneless, skinless chicken breasts
- 1/2 teaspoon kosher salt
- ½ teaspoon onion powder
- ¼ teaspoon black pepper

Preparation

1. Place the chicken breasts on a cutting board and cover with a large sheet of plastic wrap. With a rolling pin, meat mallet, or your palm, lightly crush to an even thickness.
2. To dry the brine: place the chicken on a plate and sprinkle it with kosher salt. Refrigerate uncovered for at least 30 minutes or up to 1 day - if not making dry brine, skip this step.
3. When you're ready to air fry: Take the chicken out of the fridge and let it sit at room temperature for 15 minutes.
4. In a small bowl, combine the paprika, garlic powder, onion powder, and black pepper (if you didn't brine the chicken, add the salt now).
5. Place the chicken in a large bowl and drizzle with olive oil. Sprinkle the spice mix on top. Toss to coat the chicken, making sure to rub the spices evenly on both sides.

Asparagus

Servings: 4

Ingredients

- 2 teaspoons olive oil
- Salt or to taste
- Ground black pepper or to taste
- 1 pound asparagus (about 1 bunch)
- Grated parmesan cheese optional

Preparation

1. Wash the asparagus and dry them properly.
2. Cut off the white and woody ends from the bottom.
3. Add them to a large salad bowl and drizzle with olive oil.
4. Sprinkle with salt and pepper. Mix well. (Make sure each spear is evenly coated with oil.)
5. Place seasoned asparagus in fryer basket and spread evenly.
6. Preheat your air fryer by setting the temperature to 140 C.
7. When the fryer is ready, take out the basket. Distribute the asparagus evenly in the basket.
8. Replace the basket and set the timer for 8 minutes.
9. After 4 minutes, take out the basket and carefully turn the asparagus.
10. Return basket to air fryer and check every minute until cooked through.

Crispy Potato Chips

Ingredients

- 3 medium potatoes (Yukon gold or Russet)
- Cooking spray
- Salt to taste

Preparation

1. Wash the potato and peel the skin.
2. Cut the potato into thin rounds using a mandolin or a very sharp knife. Try to cut them about 1/8 inch thick.
3. Soak the potato slices in cold water for about 30 minutes. Then, drain them and rinse them several times to remove the starch.
4. On a flat surface, lay out a layer of paper towel, then place the potato slices on top in a single layer. Add another layer of paper towel to dry the potato slices. Let them sit for 10-15 minutes until the slices are completely dry.
5. Preheat the air fryer to 150°C. It usually takes about 3 minutes to be ready.
6. Spray cooking spray on both sides of potato slices. Add the potato slices to the air fryer basket, trying to distribute them evenly. (If cooking more than one potato, cook them in batches and only add about 30 slices at a time)
7. Set the timer for 16 minutes. After 8 minutes, take out the basket and gently shake the chips. Use tongs to separate the shavings stuck to each other.
8. Put the basket back in place, and after another 8 minutes, take the basket out again and shake.
9. Now increase the temperature to 200°C and set the timer for 5 minutes. Return the basket. Watch very closely and check every 2 minutes until the fries are crispy and golden around the edges. If there are only a few soft center fries, put them back and cook for another 2 minutes.
10. Sprinkle with salt or seasoning of your choice.

Baked Potato

Servings: 4

Ingredients

- ¼ teaspoon sea salt
- ½ teaspoon garlic powder optional, but recommended
- 2 medium russet potatoes scrubbed clean
- ¼ teaspoon black pepper optional, but recommended

Optional Toppings:
- vegan bacon bits
- cashew cream
- vegan butter or margarine
- guacamole

Preparation

1. Rinse and scrub your potatoes, poke a few holes with a fork or knife all around, then sprinkle them evenly with the seasoning on all sides.
2. Place it in the basket of your deep fryer.
3. Air fry at 200 C for 35-45 minutes, flipping around the 20 minutes mark. (Use tongs to turn them over.)
4. Serve hot with one of your favorite toppings.

Brussels Sprouts

Servings: 4

Ingredients

Brussels sprouts:
- 1/4 teaspoon kosher salt
- 1/4 teaspoon black pepper
- 1 pound Brussels sprouts
- 2 teaspoons extra virgin olive oil
- 3 cloves garlic thinly sliced (optional but delish!)

Optional toppings:
- Drizzle pomegranate molasses
- 2 teaspoons pure maple syrup
- 1 tablespoon balsamic glaze or reduced balsamic vinegar
- 3 tablespoons freshly grated Parmesan cheese

Preparation

1. Trim the ends of the Brussels sprouts and remove the brown outer leaves. Cut them in half from the stem to the end. If some are very large, quarter them from stem to end so that all pieces are fairly similar in size and cook evenly.
2. OPTIONAL—This step ensures the Brussels sprouts are a little softer in the middle; that said, if you don't mind firmer sprouts, you can sauté them - I like my Brussels sprouts firm/tender on the inside and crispy on the outside, so I usually sauté them - Place Brussels sprouts in a large bowl and cover with a hot tap of water. Let stand 10 minutes.
3. A bowl of chopped vegetables in water
4. Preheat the air fryer to 160 C degrees, according to the manufacturer's instructions (for my air fryer, it's 3 minutes preheat).
5. Drain the Brussels sprouts and with a towel, pat them dry. Wipe out the bowl you used for soaking, then add the Brussels sprouts to it (if you didn't soak the sprouts, just place them in a large mixing bowl). Drizzle with oil and sprinkle with salt and black pepper. Toss to evenly coat, then add to your air fryer basket.
6. Cut Brussels sprouts in a bowl
7. Cook the sprouts for 5 minutes, then slide the basket out and shake to mix the Brussels sprouts together to encourage even cooking. Cook for another 5 minutes, then slide the basket back in. The Brussels sprouts should look crispy and almost done (if not, let them cook for a minute or more). Add the garlic cloves and stir to coat once more. Cook an additional 2 to 4 minutes, checking and shaking the basket often, until the Brussels sprouts are crispy.
8. Raw Brussels sprouts in an air fryer
9. If adding toppings, transfer the Brussels sprouts to a serving bowl (or wipe out the mixing bowl you used earlier) and stir in the desired toppings. Enjoy hot.

Potato Wedges

Servings: 4

Ingredients

- 1 teaspoon Kosher salt
- 1 teaspoon crushed rosemary
- 1 teaspoon crushed thyme leaves (if using ground, only use ¼ to ½ teaspoon)
- 2 russet potatoes (rinsed and dried)
- 1 teaspoon olive oil
- Cooking spray (optional)

Preparation

1. Cut the potatoes in half, then cut them into wedges. Each potato should make 6-8 wedges depending on the thickness of the potatoes and the desired size of the wedge.
2. In a large bowl, toss the potatoes with the seasonings and olive oil.
3. Spray the air fryer basket with cooking spray. Add the potatoes and, if desired, spray the potatoes with cooking spray for an extra crispy potato wedge.
4. Set the temperature to 390 degrees Fahrenheit and the timer to 15 minutes for normal sized wedges, adjust the time by a minute or two if the wedges are thinner or thicker.
5. Want extra crispy wedges? Raise the heat to 200°C for an additional 2-3 minutes at the end of cooking.
6. Serve immediately.

Fried Tofu

Servings: 4

Ingredients

- 1 Tbsp toasted sesame oil 15 mL
- 1 Tbsp olive oil 15 mL
- 1 16-oz block extra-firm tofu 453 g
- 2 Tbsp soy sauce 30 mL
- 1 clove garlic minced

Preparation

1. Press the tofu for at least 15 minutes, either using a tofu press or placing a heavy pan over it and letting the moisture drain out. When you're done, cut the tofu into bite-sized blocks and transfer to a bowl.
2. Combine all remaining ingredients in a small bowl. Drizzle over tofu and toss to coat. Let the tofu marinate for another 15 minutes.
3. Pour the marinade over the tofu pieces.
4. Preheat your air fryer to 190 C.
5. Add tofu blocks to your air fryer basket in a single layer.
6. Cook for 10 to 15 minutes, shaking the pan occasionally to promote even cooking.

Healthy Salmon

Servings: 4

Ingredients

- 1 teaspoon garlic powder
- ½ teaspoon paprika
- Salt and pepper to taste
- 4 salmon fillets 6 ounces each
- 1 tablespoon olive oil
- Lemon wedges for serving
- Tartar sauce for serving

Preparation

1. Preheat the air fryer to 200°C.
2. Rub each fillet with olive oil and season with garlic powder, paprika, salt and pepper.
3. Place the salmon in the air fryer and air fry for 7-9 minutes, depending on the thickness of the salmon.
4. Please note that the time may vary between air fryers.
5. Open the basket and check the desired doneness with a fork.
6. You can flip the salmon for another 1 or 2 minutes if needed.

Buffalo Cauliflower Bites

Servings: 4

Ingredients

- 2 teaspoon garlic powder
- 1 teaspoon paprika
- 0.5 teaspoon salt
- 0.25 teaspoon black pepper
- 1 head cauliflower (cut into florets)
- 100 g all-purpose flour
- 100 g water
- 100 g buffalo sauce
- optional cooking spray

For Serving:
- blue cheese dressing or ranch
- celery and carrots sticks

Preparation

1. Clean the cauliflower and cut the florets into 2-inch pieces.
2. In a large mixing bowl, whisk together the flour, garlic powder, paprika, salt, pepper, buffalo sauce and water.
3. Add the cauliflower florets to the batter. Mix to coat.
4. Spread the cauliflower on the air fryer basket. (Spray with optional cooking spray).
5. Air fry at 160°C for 15 minutes. Shake twice during the process and cook until they begin to brown. Brush with more sauce if needed.
6. Serve hot with blue cheese dressing, celery and carrots if desired.

Healthy Eggplant

Servings: 4

Ingredients

- 4 tablespoons olive oil, see note
- 2 tablespoon minced garlic, or 1 teaspoon garlic powder
- 4 pounds eggplant, 2 medium eggplants
- Salt, to taste (I used 1/2 teaspoon sea salt)
- 0.5 teaspoon black pepper

Garnishes – Optional:

- Fresh parsley, finely minced
- Parmesan cheese, grated

Preparation

1. Cut the stem off the eggplant and peel the skin if desired (see note).
2. Then, cut them into 2-inch pieces (although they may look big, they will shrink about half as they cook).
3. In a medium bowl, add the garlic, oil, salt and pepper as well as the eggplant pieces.
4. Mix with a large spoon or your hands to evenly coat.
5. Put the eggplant in your fryer basket and cook at 180 C for 15 minutes.
6. Halfway through cooking, remove the basket and shake a few times to promote even browning before continuing to cook.
7. Remove the eggplant from the air fryer and garnish with parsley and optional parmesan cheese before serving.

Quick Broccoli

Servings: 4

Ingredients

- 2 tablespoons extra virgin olive oil
- ¼ tsp garlic powder
- ¼ tsp onion powder
- 12 oz fresh broccoli florets, cut/torn into toughly even, very-small pieces
- ⅛ tsp kosher salt
- ⅛ tsp freshly ground black pepper

Optional garnishes: fresh lemon slices, freshly grated parmesan cheese

Preparation

1. Season: Combine all ingredients in a bowl; mix well to incorporate the seasonings into the broccoli florets
2. Prepare the pan: Pour 1 TB of water into the bottom of the air fryer pan (this helps prevent the contents from smoking.)
3. Cooking: Evenly add broccoli mixture to air fryer basket. Set at 200 C for 6 minutes. Once the timer goes off, immediately remove the basket and serve.
4. (Optional: sprinkle with a squeeze of fresh lemon juice or freshly grated parmesan cheese.)

Blooming onion (vegan)

Servings: 4

Ingredients

- 2 tablespoons tapioca starch
- 2 teaspoons paprika
- 1 teaspoon salt
- 1/4 teaspoon black pepper
- 1 large onion
- 70 g blanched almond flour + 2 tablespoons reserved for sprinkling
- 1/2 teaspoon garlic powder
- 1/2 teaspoon dried oregano
- 1/2 cup water

Preparation

1. Cut the top off the onions, leaving the bottom end with the roots intact. Place the onion root side up on a cutting board.
2. Make vertical cuts all the way down around the onion to form small strips. Be sure to leave the onion attached at the root. You want the onion to "unfurl" to form this blooming, but still attached, onion shape.
3. Add the onion to cold water and soak for 1 hour. This will help plump up the lumps and also help distribute them better. Remove from water and pat dry.
4. In a bowl, add the remaining ingredients, except for the additional 2 tablespoons of almond flour. Stir in the water to form a thick paste.
5. Coat the whole onion in the batter. Sprinkle with the remaining 2 tablespoons of almond flour.
6. Coat the bottom of the air fryer with cooking spray and place the onion inside, root side down. Spray with cooking spray.
7. Bake for 25 minutes at 180°C.

Corn on the cob

Servings: 4

Ingredients

- 2 tbsp unsalted butter melted
- 4 Corn on the Cob
- 1 tsp salt
- 1 tsp pepper

Preparation

1. Rinse the corn and pat it dry.
2. Brush each cob of corn with melted butter. Then season with salt and pepper, to taste.
3. Place the corn in the air fryer basket or on the shelf.
4. Air fry at 200°C for 12 minutes, turning the corn halfway through cooking.

Frozen Tater Tots

Servings: 4

Ingredients

- Frozen Tater Tots
- Seasoning – Cajun Seasoning (optional)

Preparation

1. Spray the air fryer basket with nonstick.
2. Place the frozen tater tots in an even layer in the air fryer basket. Season.
3. Air fry at 200C for 8-12 minutes or until tots are crispiness.
4. Stir once during cooking.

Zucchini Chips

Servings: 4

Ingredients

- 1 tablespoon apple cider vinegar
- 2 teaspoon seasoned salt
- 600 g of zucchini, sliced thin
- nonstick oil spray
- 1 teaspoon garlic powder

Preparation

1. Using a mandolin or chef's knife, cut the zucchini into thin slices.
2. Place zucchini in a mixing bowl. Add the vinegar and stir to combine.
3. Spray the air fryer basket with nonstick cooking spray.
4. Add the zucchini chips in a single layer to the air fryer basket.
5. Air fry at 180°C for 4-5 minutes. Flip the fries and fry for an additional 4-5 minutes, until they reach the desired crispiness.
6. Check for chips frequently and remove them early if they start to burn.
7. When finished frying, sprinkle with seasoned salt and garlic powder.

Air Fryer Okra

Servings: 4

Ingredients

- 160 g okra (fresh)
- 1 egg
- 1 teaspoon water
- 1 tablespoon flour
- 70 g bread crumbs
- 1 tablespoon olive oil or coconut oil

Preparation

1. In a small bowl, whisk together the egg and 1 teaspoon water, set aside.
2. Rinse the okra and cut off the top and bottom.
3. Cut into pieces about 1/4 inch thick. Mix the okra in the flour. Then dip each piece in the egg mixture, then in the breadcrumbs.
4. Air fry at 170 C for 6 minutes.
5. Depending on the size of your air fryer, you'll probably need to do this in two batches.
6. Mix the breaded okra in the oil (melt the coconut oil into a liquid if necessary).
7. Then air fry for another 2-3 minutes.

Homemade pizza rolls

Ingredients

- 1 pound pizza dough (or 1 can refrigerated pizza dough)
- 2 teaspoons olive oil
- 100 g pizza sauce (plus more for dipping)
- 200 g mozzarella cheese
- 100 g pepperoni

Toppings:
- Parmesan cheese
- Chopped parsley for garnish

Preparation

1. Roll out the dough into a 10×14 inch rectangle. (You can use homemade or store-bought dough for this recipe).
2. Brush the surface with olive oil.
3. Spread pizza sauce evenly over dough. (Leave about 1 inch space around the edges).
4. Top with pepperoni and mozzarella.
5. Roll the dough into a tight sausage, starting at the long end.
6. Place the log seam side down and cut into 1 inch slices. (You can place the log on a baking sheet in the fridge to cool for about 20 minutes. This will make slicing much easier, and it's an optional step.)
7. Place the pizza rolls in the basket and arrange them about 1/2 inch apart. (you will need to cook in batches if necessary.)
8. Set the temperature to 160 °C and set the time to 8 minutes.
9. After 8 minutes, check every 1 minute until the cheese has melted and the dough is cooked through.

Hard boiled eggs

Servings: 4

Ingredients

- 8 eggs
- Seasoning such as salt and pepper optional

Preparation

1. Remove the eggs from the refrigerator and place them directly into the air fryer basket.
2. Set the temperature to 140 °C. You do not need to preheat the air fryer.
3. Cook for 15 minutes if you prefer a hard-boiled egg with a softer yolk.
4. For soft-boiled eggs, cook for 11-14 minutes and for hard-boiled eggs, cook for 17 minutes. See photos and details in the post.
5. Once cooked, remove them from the basket and place them in a bowl of ice water or run them under cold water for about 5 minutes.
6. Take off right away and enjoy!

Mozzarella Sticks

Servings: 4

Ingredients

- ⅛ teaspoon kosher salt, or to taste
- ⅛ teaspoon ground black pepper
- 2 large eggs, divided
- 50g panko or bread crumbs
- ½ teaspoon Italian seasoning
- 170g mozzarella string cheese (6 cheese sticks, each one cut in half)
- 2 tablespoons whole wheat or all-purpose flour
- ¼ teaspoon garlic powder
- Olive oil spray
- Marinara or ranch, or for dipping

Preparation

1. Place the cut mozzarella sticks in a zip lock bag and freeze until frozen, at least 1 hour.
2. Prepare three small, shallow bowls. In first bowl, combine flour, salt and pepper; mix lightly.
3. In the second bowl, add 1 egg and beat lightly.
4. In the third bowl, combine the panko, Italian seasoning and garlic powder.
5. One at a time, coat the mozzarella pieces in the flour mixture, then dip them in the beaten egg and finally coat them in the panko mixture, pressing lightly to adhere the coating.
6. Place on a baking sheet lined with parchment paper and freeze again for 30 minutes.
7. RESERVE the breadcrumbs. In a small, shallow bowl, beat the second egg.
8. Remove the mozzarella sticks from the freezer and dip them in the egg, then coat them again in the breadcrumb mixture.
9. Return to freezer for another 30 minutes (see note).
10. Heat the air fryer to 200 C. Place the breaded mozzarella sticks in a single layer and spray with olive oil. (You'll need to do these in batches - don't pile them up or overcrowd the basket!)
11. Air fry for 5-6 minutes or until golden brown.

Crispy Frozen French Fries Without Oil

Servings: 4

Ingredients

- 500 g frozen French fries (I used unseasoned fries, if yours are already seasoned, skip the salt and pepper)
- Salt to taste
- Pepper to taste

Preparation

1. Preheat your air fryer by setting the temperature to 200 C. (It usually takes about 3 minutes to preheat an air fryer.)
2. In a large bowl, season the frozen fries with salt and pepper.
3. When the fryer is ready, take out the basket.
4. Distribute the frozen fries evenly in the basket, overlapping them as little as possible. (You will need to cook in batches.)
5. Replace the basket and set the timer for 13 minutes.
6. After 6 minutes, take out the basket and shake the fries.
7. Return the basket to the air fryer. After 4 more minutes, check every 2 minutes until golden brown and crispy.
8. Season with more salt and pepper if needed.
9. Let the fries cool slightly before serving. They will become more crispy as they cool.
10. Serve with your favorite dip and enjoy!

Sweet Potato Fries

Servings: 4

Ingredients

- 2 teaspoons olive oil
- ½ teaspoon salt
- ¼ teaspoon garlic powder
- 2 medium sweet potatoes peeled
- ¼ teaspoon paprika
- ⅛ teaspoon black pepper

Preparation

1. Preheat the air fryer to 190 C. Peel the sweet potatoes, then cut each potato into ¼-inch-thick sticks.
2. Place the sweet potatoes in a large mixing bowl and toss with the olive oil, salt, garlic powder, paprika and black pepper.
3. Cook in 2 or 3 batches, depending on the size of your basket without overloading the pan, until crispy. I recommend 12 minutes, turning halfway through. This may vary depending on your air fryer.
4. Serve immediately with your favorite dip.

Air Fried Bacon

Servings: 4

Ingredients

- 4 strips bacon thick or thin, cut in half crosswise

- Black pepper optional

Preparation

1. Wipe out your air fryer to prevent the bacon from smoking. Preheat the air fryer to 170°C. If you want to keep the bacon warm between batches, preheat your oven to 110°C.
2. Slide out your air fryer basket. Using tongs, arrange the halved bacon slices in a single layer.
3. Make sure they don't overlap (a little touching around the edges is OK). If desired, sprinkle with black pepper. Depending on the size of your basket and how many strips you want to cook at once, you may need to cook the bacon in batches.
4. Cook the bacon for 5 minutes (for thinner bacon) or up to 9 minutes (for thicker bacon), until it reaches the desired crispiness. The bacon will wrap around crispy. Frequently check the progress of the bacon to make sure it is not burning.
5. Transfer the bacon to a plate lined with paper towel and blot lightly. If desired, transfer the bacon to a baking sheet and store in the oven.
6. For other batches: repeat with the remaining bacon (no need to wipe out the air fryer in between unless it starts to smoke, in which case carefully pour out the fat and wipe it out with a paper towel). Enjoy!

Air fried steak

Ingredients

- 2 tsp salt (plus more to taste)
- 2 tsp black pepper (plus more to taste)
- 2 strip loin steaks (1.25" thick; or use any steaks of your choosing)
- 2 Tbsp butter (melted)

Preparation

1. Sprinkle the steaks with salt and pepper, place them on a plate and refrigerate for 2-3 days, uncovered. Turn every 12 hours or so, blotting up any juices with a paper towel.
2. This step is recommended for superior tenderness and improved flavor, but you can skip it if you're pressed for time.
3. Take the steaks out of the refrigerator 45 to 60 minutes before cooking and let them come to room temperature.
4. Brush the steaks with melted butter on both sides, place them on the rack of your air fryer. Cook at 200 C for 15 minutes, without preheating, for medium cooking.
5. Cook about 1-2 minutes less for medium-rare and rare respectively, and 1-2 minutes more for medium-rare and well-done respectively. Times will need to be adjusted further if air frying thicker or thinner steaks than 1.25" thick.
6. These cooking times are approximate, so use an instant-read thermometer in conjunction with the chart in the Notes section.
7. Remove the steaks from the air fryer, wrap them in foil or waxed paper and let rest for 10 minutes, then serve. Try serving with compound butter, it will add a ton of flavor.

Air fryer shrimp

Ingredients

- 680 grams raw Shrimp - peeled and deveined
- 1 tablespoon Oil - extra virgin, coconut, or avocado
- ½ tablespoon of Seasoning - Cajun, Lemon Pepper, Salt and Pepper, or Old Bay

Preparation

1. Pat the shrimp dry with paper towel to remove any excess moisture.
2. Toss the shrimp in the cooking oil and seasonings - you can do this step in the air fryer basket or in a separate bowl.
3. Place the prawns in a single layer and cook at 200 C for 5 minutes for medium prawns or 10-15 minutes for jumbo.
4. Shrimp are fully cooked when they turn opaque.
5. Serve immediately or store in the fridge for 2-3 days.

Meatloaf

Ingredients

- ½ tsp. salt
- ¼ tsp. pepper
- 1 egg, lightly beaten
- ½ small onion, finely chopped
- 50 g dry breadcrumbs
- 2 Tbsp. ketchup, divided
- 1 tsp. Worcestershire sauce
- 1 tsp. Italian seasoning
- ½ tsp. garlic powder
- 500 g lean ground beef
- 1 Tbsp. yellow mustard

Preparation

1. In a large bowl, combine 1 tablespoon ketchup, Worcestershire sauce, Italian seasoning, garlic powder, salt, pepper and egg.
2. Mix the onion then the breadcrumbs. Once well mixed, add the ground beef.
3. Use your hands to evenly mix the meat with the egg mixture, being careful not to overmix as overmixing will make it difficult.
4. Shape the meat into a 4×6 inch loaf 2 inches high. Turn the air fryer to 150 C and place the bread in the air fryer.
5. Cook for 15 minutes at 150°C.
6. Meanwhile, in a small bowl, combine the remaining tablespoon of ketchup and the mustard.
7. Remove meatloaf from oven and spread with mustard mixture.
8. Return the meatloaf to the air fryer and continue to cook at 150°C until an instant-read thermometer inserted into the loaf reads 72°C, about 8-10 minutes more.
9. Once the meatloaf has reached 72°C, remove the air fryer basket from the fryer and allow the loaf to sit in the basket for 5-10 minutes.
10. Transfer the meatloaf to a cutting board and cut into 3/4" to 1" slices.

Burritos

Servings: 4

Ingredients

- 2-3 frozen burritos (breakfast or lunch burritos)
- Aluminum foil

Preparation

1. Wrap each frozen burrito in foil.
2. Preheat the air fryer by setting the temperature to 180 C. (It may take about 3 minutes to preheat some air fryers. Other air fryers do not require preheating time.)
3. Place the wrapped burritos in the air fryer basket.
4. Replace the basket and set the timer for 40 minutes. (Smaller burritos can take 30 minutes to cook, and larger ones can take upwards of 40 minutes.)
5. Flip the burritos after 20 minutes.
6. Gently remove the burritos with kitchen tongs. Let it cool down a bit before unpacking it. Be careful that the burritos are piping hot right out of the air fryer.

Hamburgers

Servings: 4

Ingredients

- 1 - 1 1/4 pounds ground chuck (80/20 ground beef)
- 1 Tbsp Worchestershire sauce
- 1 tsp salt
- 1/2 tsp black pepper
- 4 hamburger buns
- 4 slices cheese (optional)

Preparation

1. Preheat the air fryer to 180 C.
2. Meanwhile, combine ground beef, salt, pepper and Worcestershire sauce. Mix until everything is just combined, do not over mix.
3. Divide the meat into 4 equal portions and form 4 patties. Use your thumb to make a slit in the center of each patty.
4. Place the patties in the air fryer basket, making sure they are not touching. Cook for 8 minutes, turning halfway through.
5. If you're topping with cheese, add slices after the 8 minutes, then return for an additional minute to let it melt.

Crispy Air Fried Fish

Servings: 4

Ingredients

- 2 teaspoons Cajun seasoning
- ½ teaspoon paprika
- ½ teaspoon garlic powder
- 2 tablespoons cornmeal
- Sea salt flakes to taste
- 2 white fish fillets
- Low calorie spray

Preparation

1. Preheat the air fryer to 200C.
2. Mix the first 5 ingredients together then add to a Ziploc bag.
3. Rinse the catfish, pat it dry and add the fillets to the Ziploc bag.
4. Close the bag and shake until the fillets are completely coated.
5. Place in air fryer basket. (If you have a small fryer, you will need to cook them one at a time).
6. Spray the fillets with a low-calorie spray, close the air fryer and cook for 10 minutes.
7. Flip and cook for an additional 3-4 minutes, or until cooked through.

Onion Rings

Servings: 4

Ingredients

- 1 egg
- 60 g panko breadcrumbs
- 2 Tbsp olive oil
- 1 large yellow sweet onion, sliced
- 60 g all-purpose flour
- 1 tsp paprika
- 1 tsp salt, divided
- 120 ml buttermilk, see tips above for making your own
- 1/2-inch thick and separated into rings
- Oil Spray, optional

Preparation

1. You need 4 shallow bowls or deep plates. In the first, mix the flour, paprika and ½ teaspoon of salt. In the second bowl, combine the buttermilk (or milk and vinegar/lemon juice) and egg, then add ¼ cup of the flour mixture from the first bowl.
2. In the third, combine the panko breadcrumbs, ½ tsp salt and olive oil with a fork, until the oil is evenly distributed. Put half of the panko in a fourth bowl so you can move on to the second part after the first becomes sticky.
3. Pat the onion rings dry with paper towel to remove excess moisture. Using a fork, dredge the onion rings in the flour mixture, drop them in the buttermilk mixture then dredge them in the panko mixture. (TIP: Freeze the breaded onion rings for 15 minutes on a baking sheet, this helps the panko mixture stick better.)
4. Spray the air fryer basket with oil spray. Place the onion rings in a single layer in the air fryer basket. You can place smaller rings inside larger rings if needed, just make sure there is space between them.
5. Bake at 200 C until golden and crispy, about 11-15 minutes. Spray with cooking spray after about 6 minutes. You don't need to turn the onion rings.
6. Gently lift the onion rings with a spatula or cookie fork and serve.

Crispy tortilla chips

Servings: 4

Ingredients

- 12 small tortillas corn or flour (6-inch)
- cooking spray
- salt to taste

Preparation

1. Preheat your air fryer by setting the temperature to 170 C. (It usually takes about 3 minutes to preheat an air fryer.)
2. Spray your tortillas with cooking spray on each side and season with salt to taste.
3. Place 6 tortillas in a stack and cut them in half. Then cut each half into 3 small triangles (see photos in post).
4. When the fryer is ready, take out the basket. Spread the tortilla pieces in the basket in a single layer, overlapping them as little as possible. (You will have to cook in batches. I was able to fit 9 pieces in the basket each time.)
5. Replace the basket and set the timer for 5 minutes.
6. After 3 minutes, take out the basket and gently stir and flip the chips.
7. Return basket to air fryer and cook 2 minutes more or until golden brown and crispy.
8. Salt again if necessary.
9. Let the tortilla chips cool before serving. They will become more crispy as they cool.

Quick and Easy Meatballs

Servings: 4

Ingredients

- 4 garlic cloves peeled
- 50 g parsley roughly chopped
- 2 eggs lightly beaten
- 100 g Italian seasoned breadcrumbs
- 100 g crumbled feta cheese
- 500 g ground beef
- 500 g ground pork
- 1 medium onion peeled and roughly chopped
- 1 Tablespoon Worcestershire sauce
- 1 teaspoon salt
- 1/2 teaspoon black pepper

Preparation

1. Blend the onion, garlic cloves and parsley in a mini food processor.
2. Process until finely chopped. Put aside.
3. In a large bowl, place ground beef, ground pork, onion mixture, eggs, Italian seasoned breadcrumbs, feta cheese, Worcestershire sauce, salt and black pepper. Use hands to mix until combined.
4. Take 2 tablespoons of meat mixture and roll it into a ball. Repeat with meat mixture so all meatballs are rolled.
5. Place the meatballs in the air fryer basket in a single layer making sure the meatballs are not touching each other.
6. Place basket in air fryer and cook at 200°C for 10-12 minutes or until internal temperature reaches 72°C.

Tilapia without Breading

Servings: 4

Ingredients

- 4 teaspoons olive oil
- 4 teaspoons fresh chives chopped
- 4 teaspoons fresh parsley chopped
- 2 teaspoon minced garlic
- 4 fresh tilapia filets approximately 6 oz each
- freshly ground pepper to taste
- salt to taste

Preparation

1. Preheat the air fryer to 200C.
2. Pat the fresh tilapia fillets dry with paper towel.
3. In a small bowl, combine olive oil, chives, parsley, garlic, salt and pepper.
4. Brush the top of the tilapia fillets.
5. Brush the bottom of the basket with a little olive oil or spray with cooking spray.
6. Bake 8 to 10 minutes or until fish flakes easily with a fork and is no longer translucent. (At least 62 C is recommended by the FDA)
7. Serve immediately.

Zucchini Chips

Servings: 4

Ingredients

- 1 tablespoon apple cider vinegar
- 2 teaspoon seasoned salt
- 600 g of zucchini, sliced thin
- nonstick oil spray
- 1 teaspoon garlic powder

Preparation

1. Using a mandolin or chef's knife, cut the zucchini into thin slices.
2. Place zucchini in a mixing bowl. Add the vinegar and stir to combine.
3. Spray the air fryer basket with nonstick cooking spray.
4. Add the zucchini chips in a single layer to the air fryer basket.
5. Air fry at 160°C for 4-5 minutes. Flip the fries and fry for an additional 4-5 minutes, until they reach the desired crispiness.
6. Check for chips frequently and remove them early if they start to burn.
7. When finished frying, sprinkle with seasoned salt and garlic powder.

Garlic Parmesan Carrot Fries

Servings: 4

Ingredients

- 50 g Parmesan cheese
- 1 Tbsp olive oil
- 2 tsp garlic powder
- 1 tsp salt
- 1 tsp pepper
- 3 medium carrots, cleaned and scrubbed
- 100 g bread crumbs
- 1 Tbsp fresh parsley, chopped
- splash lemon juice

Preparation

1. Preheat the Air Fryer to 200C.
2. Cut the carrots in half. Then cut each half into several thin strips.
3. Combine breadcrumbs, Parmesan, garlic powder, salt and pepper in a shallow dish.
4. Fry the carrot strips in olive oil. Then place in breadcrumbs and cheese mixture and coat.
5. Place carrot fries on a parchment-lined cookie sheet and bake for 15-20 minutes or until golden brown and crispy.
6. Remove from oven and garnish with parsley, a pinch of salt and a squeeze of lemon juice.
7. Serve hot and enjoy!

Roasted Potatoes

Servings: 4

Ingredients

- 1 teaspoon sea salt
- 1 teaspoon black pepper
- 2 tsp Cajun seasoning (optional)
- 1 pound petite Yukon or gold potatoes
- 1 pound petite red potatoes
- 2-3 T olive oil

Optional to add during cooking:

- 2-3 large cloves of garlic, smashed
- 1 large bunch of fresh thyme

Optional after cooking:

- 1-2 large spoonfuls of whole grain or country Dijon mustard

Preparation

1. Preheat the air fryer to 200 C for 10 minutes.
2. While the air fryer preheats, cut the potatoes in half lengthwise at the thickest part.
3. Once the potatoes have been cut, rinse them quickly under cold water and let them drain well in a colander.
4. Combine potatoes, olive oil, salt, pepper and Cajun seasoning in large bowl; toss or stir to evenly coat the potatoes.
5. Once the air fryer is preheated, add the seasoned potatoes to the air fryer basket. If using, add crushed garlic and thyme sprigs.
6. Air fry at 200°C for 10 minutes. After 10 minutes, stir the potatoes. Bake at 200C for an additional 8-12 minutes until the potatoes are roasted, crispy and fork tender.
7. Remove potatoes to a large serving bowl, removing sprigs of garlic and thyme, if using. Taste for seasoning and add more salt or pepper if desired.
8. Optionally, once cooked, you can add whole-grain or country-style Dijon mustard to the serving bowl and toss lightly.

Stuffed peppers

Servings: 4

Ingredients

- 1 15 ounce can of diced tomatoes
- 1 8 ounce can of tomato sauce
- 400 g rice cooked
- 1 Tablespoon Italian Seasoning
- 1 teaspoon garlic powder
- 4 whole bell peppers
- 1 tablespoon olive oil
- 1 small onion diced
- 1 pound lean ground beef
- Salt and pepper
- 2 cups Colby Jack cheese shredded

Preparation

1. To prepare peppers, cut off the top and remove any veins or seeds inside. In a medium saucepan over medium-high heat, add the olive oil and onion.
2. Cook until almost tender. Add ground beef and cook and crumble until no longer pink.
3. Add diced tomatoes, tomato sauce, rice, Italian seasoning, garlic powder, salt and pepper.
4. Stuff the peppers with the mixture and place them in the basket of the air fryer.
5. Bake peppers at 170 until tender for 10 minutes.
6. Top with cheese then cook for another 2-3 minutes.

Crispy Tofu

Ingredients

- 1 teaspoon paprika
- ½ teaspoon sea salt
- 2 teaspoons cornstarch
- ½ tablespoon light soy sauce, or liquid aminos
- 1 lb block of extra firm tofu, pressed for 30 minutes then cut into 1" cubes, (16 oz.)
- 1 teaspoon garlic powder
- ½ teaspoon onion powder
- ½ teaspoon sesame oil or any oil
- ¼ teaspoon ground black pepper

Preparation

1. In a medium-sized bowl, place the pressed and cubed tofu. Add the liquid amino acids and mix well to coat.
2. Add all other seasoning ingredients, including the oil, and toss to combine.
3. Place them in your air fryer in a single row, so that all of the tofu has some space around each piece.
4. Set your air fryer to 200 C. Cook for 10 minutes, shaking the basket after 5 minutes, then continue cooking.
5. Remove after cooking the tofu.
6. Leave to cool for a few minutes then serve.
7. Enjoy!

Nachos

Servings: 4

Ingredients

- 2 oz tortilla chips (about 30 thin tortilla chips)
- ½ teaspoon taco seasoning
- 100 g canned black beans, rinsed and drained
- 100 g shredded Mexican blend cheese

Optional toppings:
- Light sour cream
- Guacamole
- Pico de gallo
- Fresh cilantro

Preparation

1. Lightly spray the bottom of the air fryer basket with nonstick spray.
2. Place the tortilla chips in a single layer in the air fryer basket.
3. Lightly sprinkle tortilla chips with taco seasoning. Add black beans (or other meat) and top with grated cheese.
4. Air fry at 150°C for 3-4 minutes, until the cheese is melted and just starting to brown on the edge.
5. Add toppings as desired and serve hot!

Crispy Eggplant Parmesan

Servings: 4

Ingredients

- 1 tsp Italian seasoning mix
- 3 tablespoon whole wheat flour
- 1 egg + 1 tablespoon water
- olive oil spray
- 200 g marinara sauce
- 1 large eggplant mine was around 1.25 lb
- ½ cup whole wheat bread crumbs
- 3 tablespoon finely grated parmesan cheese
- salt to taste
- 50 g grated mozzarella cheese
- Fresh parsley or basil to garnish

Preparation

1. Cut the eggplant into slices of about ½". Rub a little salt on both sides of the slices and leave it on for at least 10-15 minutes.
2. Meanwhile, in a small bowl, mix the egg with the water and flour to prepare the batter.
3. In a medium shallow dish, combine the breadcrumbs, Parmesan cheese, Italian seasoning mix and a little salt. Mix well.
4. Now apply the paste evenly on each slice of eggplant. Dip the breaded slices in the breadcrumb mixture to coat them evenly on all sides. See the useful tips section above to perform this task perfectly.
5. Place breaded eggplant slices on a clean, dry flat plate and spray with oil. See the notes section for more details.
6. Preheat the Air Fryer to 170 C. Then place the eggplant slices on the grill and cook for about 8 min.
7. Top the air fried slices with about 1 tablespoon marinara sauce and lightly spread some fresh mozzarella cheese on top. Cook the eggplant another 1-2 min or until the cheese melts.
8. Serve hot alongside your favorite pasta.

Chicken Nuggets

Servings: 4

Ingredients

- 2 lb boneless chicken breasts , cut into 1 – ½ inch cubes
- 100 g pickle juice
- 100 g milk
- 1 large egg

Breading:

- 200 g all-purpose flour
- 3 Tablespoons powdered sugar
- 1/2 teaspoon paprika
- 1/2 teaspoon chili powder
- 1 teaspoon freshly ground black pepper
- 1/2 teaspoon salt
- 1/2 teaspoon baking powder
- 1 – 2 teaspoons cayenne pepper *optional, for a spicy chicken nuggets

Preparation

1. Cut the chicken into 1.5 inch pieces and place in a bowl or ziplock bag with the pickle juice and marinate for 30 minutes.
2. Add flour, powdered sugar, paprika, black pepper, chili powder, salt and baking powder to a ziplock bag.
3. Add milk and egg to a separate bowl and mix. Preheat the air fryer to 170 C.
4. Remove the chicken from the pickle marinade and add it to the bowl with the egg mixture.
5. Using a spoon, scoop out the pieces (letting any excess egg mixture drip off) and place them in the ziplock bag with the dry seasonings. Seal and shake the bag to evenly coat all the chicken.
6. Spray the bottom of the frying basket with nonstick cooking spray and place half of the chicken pieces in a single layer on the bottom of the basket, spacing them apart so they don't stick together.
7. Generously spray the top of each piece of chicken with cooking spray.
8. Fry at 170°C for 6 minutes. Open the air fryer, flip the chicken pieces to the other side, and spray the tops again with cooking spray. Increase fryer temperature to 200°C and cook for 2 more minutes, or until crispy and cooked through. (Exact cooking time will vary depending on the size of your nuggets, air fryer, etc.)

Apple Chips

Ingredients

- 2 Red Apples
- Cinnamon

Preparation

1. Using the Ninja Foodi's dehydrating racks or wire racks, place at least one into the Ninja Foodi's jar.
2. Slice the apples and place them evenly on the rack, use an additional rack and stack them if necessary.
3. Close the lid that is attached to the Ninja Foodi and press the dehydrator function at 8 hours at 40 C.
4. After 8 hours, remove the apples and coat them with cinnamon, mix well and serve.
5. Store them in an airtight container.

Crispy Air Fryer Chicken Wings

Servings: 4

Ingredients

- 500g chicken wings
- 1 tsp salt
- 1 tsp black pepper
- 1 tsp garlic powder
- 2 tbsp olive oil

Preparation

1. Mix the chicken wings with salt, pepper, and garlic powder.

2. Brush with olive oil and place in the air fryer basket.

3. Cook at 200°C for 20-25 minutes, flipping halfway through.

Air Fryer Falafel

Ingredients

- 400g canned chickpeas, drained and rinsed
- 1 small onion, chopped
- 2 garlic cloves, minced
- 1 tsp ground cumin
- 1 tsp ground coriander
- 50 g chopped fresh parsley
- 1 tbsp lemon juice
- 3 tbsp all-purpose flour
- 1 tsp baking powder
- 1/2 tsp salt

Preparation

1. In the air fryer, pulse the chickpeas, onion, garlic, cumin, coriander, parsley, and lemon juice until combined but still slightly chunky.

2. Add the flour, baking powder, and salt and pulse until the mixture comes together.

3. Form the mixture into small balls and place in the air fryer basket.

4. Cook at 180°C for 12-15 minutes, flipping halfway through.

Air Fryer Chicken Tenders

Ingredients

- 500g chicken tenders
- 1 tsp salt
- 1 tsp paprika
- 1/2 tsp garlic powder
- 1/2 tsp onion powder
- 1/2 tsp dried thyme
- 1/4 tsp black pepper
- 100 g all-purpose flour
- 2 eggs, beaten
- 200 g panko breadcrumbs

Preparation

1. Mix the salt, paprika, garlic powder, onion powder, thyme, and black pepper together.

2. Coat the chicken tenders in the seasoned flour.

3. Dip the chicken tenders in the beaten eggs, then coat in the panko breadcrumbs.

4. Place the chicken tenders in the air fryer basket and cook at 200°C for 10-12 minutes, flipping halfway through.

Air Fryer Sweet Potato Fries

Servings: 4

Ingredients

- 2 large sweet potatoes, peeled and cut into fries
- 2 tbsp cornstarch
- 1 tsp paprika
- 1/2 tsp garlic powder
- 1/4 tsp onion powder
- 1/4 tsp salt
- 2 tbsp olive oil

Preparation

1. Toss the sweet potato fries with the cornstarch, paprika, garlic powder, onion powder, and salt.

2. Drizzle with olive oil and toss to coat.

3. Place the sweet potato fries in the air fryer basket and cook at 200°C for 15-20 minutes, shaking the basket every 5 minutes.

Air Fryer Salmon

Ingredients

- 2 salmon fillets
- 1 tsp olive oil
- 1 tsp salt
- 1/2 tsp garlic powder
- 1/2 tsp onion powder
- 1/4 tsp black pepper
- Lemon wedges, for serving

Preparation

1. Brush the salmon fillets with olive oil.
2. Mix the salt, garlic powder, onion powder, and black pepper together and sprinkle over the salmon fillets.
3. Place the salmon fillets in the air fryer basket and cook at 180°C for 10-12 minutes, or until cooked through.
4. Serve with lemon wedges.

Air Fryer Pork Chops

Servings: 4

Ingredients

- 4 pork chops
- 1 tsp garlic powder
- 1 tsp onion powder
- 1 tsp paprika
- 1 tsp salt
- 1/4 tsp black pepper
- 1 tbsp olive oil

Preparation

1. Mix the garlic powder, onion powder, paprika, salt, and black pepper together.

2. Rub the mixture all over the pork chops.

3. Brush the pork chops with olive oil.

4. Place the pork chops in the air fryer basket and cook at 200°C for 15-18 minutes, flipping halfway through.

Air Fryer Vegetable Spring Rolls

Servings: 4

Ingredients

- 8 spring roll wrappers
- 200 g shredded cabbage
- 200 g shredded carrots
- 100 g sliced mushrooms
- 100 g sliced bell pepper
- 2 tbsp soy sauce
- 1 tbsp cornstarch
- 1 tbsp olive oil

Preparation

1. In a large bowl, mix the cabbage, carrots, mushrooms, bell pepper, soy sauce, and cornstarch together.

2. Place a spoonful of the mixture in the center of each spring roll wrapper.

3. Roll the wrapper tightly, tucking in the sides.

4. Brush the spring rolls with olive oil.

5. Place the spring rolls in the air fryer basket and cook at 200°C for 10-12 minutes, flipping halfway through.

Air Fryer Parmesan Crusted Chicken

Servings: 4

Ingredients

- 4 boneless, skinless chicken breasts
- 100 g grated Parmesan cheese
- 100 g panko breadcrumbs
- 1 tsp garlic powder
- 1 tsp dried basil
- 1/2 tsp salt
- 1/4 tsp black pepper
- 50 g olive oil

Preparation

1. Mix the Parmesan cheese, panko breadcrumbs, garlic powder, basil, salt, and black pepper together.

2. Brush the chicken breasts with olive oil.

3. Coat the chicken breasts in the Parmesan mixture, pressing it on firmly.

4. Place the chicken breasts in the air fryer basket and cook at 200°C for 15-18 minutes, flipping halfway through.

Air Fryer Baked Potatoes

Servings: 4

Ingredients

- 4 medium potatoes
- 1 tbsp olive oil
- 1 tsp salt

Preparation

1. Scrub the potatoes and pierce them several times with a fork.

2. Rub the potatoes with olive oil and sprinkle with salt.

3. Place the potatoes in the air fryer basket and cook at 200°C for 40-45 minutes, flipping halfway through.

Air Fryer Coconut Shrimp

Servings: 4

Ingredients

- 500 g large shrimp, peeled and deveined
- 200 g shredded coconut
- 100 g panko breadcrumbs
- 50 g all-purpose flour
- 1 tsp garlic powder
- 1 tsp paprika
- 1/2 tsp salt
- 2 eggs, beaten

Preparation

1. Mix the coconut, panko breadcrumbs, flour, garlic powder, paprika, and salt together.

2. Dip the shrimp in the beaten eggs, then coat in the coconut mixture.

3. Place the shrimp in the air fryer basket and cook at 200°C for 8-10 minutes, flipping halfway through.

Air Fryer Meatballs

Servings: 4

Ingredients

- 500 g ground beef
- 100 g panko breadcrumbs
- 50 g grated Parmesan cheese
- 1 egg, beaten
- 1 tsp garlic powder
- 1 tsp onion powder
- 1/2 tsp salt
- 1/4 tsp black pepper

Preparation

1. Mix the ground beef, panko breadcrumbs, Parmesan cheese, egg, garlic powder, onion powder, salt, and black pepper together.

2. Form the mixture into small meatballs.

3. Place the meatballs in the air fryer basket and cook at 200°C for 10-12 minutes, shaking the basket halfway through.

Air Fryer Zucchini Fries

Servings: 4

Ingredients

- 2 medium zucchinis, cut into fries
- 100 g panko breadcrumbs
- 50 g grated Parmesan cheese
- 1 tsp garlic powder
- 1 tsp dried oregano
- 1/2 tsp salt
- 1/4 tsp black pepper
- 1 egg, beaten

Preparation

1. Mix the panko breadcrumbs, Parmesan cheese, garlic powder, oregano, salt, and black pepper together.

2. Dip the zucchini fries in the beaten egg, then coat in the breadcrumb mixture.

3. Place the zucchini fries in the air fryer basket and cook at 200°C for 8-10 minutes, flipping halfway through.

Air Fryer Mozzarella Sticks

Servings: 4

Ingredients

- 8 mozzarella sticks
- 100 g all-purpose flour
- 2 eggs, beaten
- 200 g panko breadcrumbs
- 1 tsp garlic powder
- 1 tsp dried oregano
- 1/2 tsp salt
- 1/4 tsp black pepper

Preparation

1. Cut the mozzarella sticks in half.

2. Place the flour, beaten eggs, and panko breadcrumbs mixed with garlic powder, oregano, salt, and black pepper in separate bowls.

3. Dip each mozzarella stick half in the flour, then the beaten egg, then the breadcrumb mixture.

4. Place the mozzarella sticks in the air fryer basket and cook at 200°C for 6-8 minutes, until crispy and golden brown.

Air Fryer Teriyaki Chicken

Servings: 4

Ingredients

- 4 boneless, skinless chicken thighs
- 50 g soy sauce
- 50 g honey
- 1 tbsp rice vinegar
- 1 tsp garlic powder
- 1 tsp ginger powder
- 1/2 tsp sesame oil
- 1/4 tsp black pepper
- Sesame seeds, for serving

Preparation

1. Mix the soy sauce, honey, rice vinegar, garlic powder, ginger powder, sesame oil, and black pepper together in a bowl.

2. Place the chicken thighs in the marinade and refrigerate for 30 minutes.

3. Place the chicken thighs in the air fryer basket and cook at 200°C for 15-18 minutes, flipping halfway through.

4. Sprinkle with sesame seeds before serving.

Air Fryer Onion Rings

Servings: 4

Ingredients

- 2 large onions, cut into rings
- 100 g all-purpose flour
- 2 eggs, beaten
- 200 g panko breadcrumbs
- 1 tsp garlic powder
- 1 tsp dried thyme
- 1/2 tsp salt
- 1/4 tsp black pepper

Preparation

1. Separate the onion rings and place the flour, beaten eggs, and panko breadcrumbs mixed with garlic powder, thyme, salt, and black pepper in separate bowls.

2. Dip each onion ring in the flour, then the beaten egg, then the breadcrumb mixture.

3. Place the onion rings in the air fryer basket and cook at 200°C for 8-10 minutes, shaking the basket halfway through.

Air Fryer BBQ Ribs

Servings: 4

Ingredients

- 1 rack baby back ribs
- 1 tsp garlic powder
- 1 tsp onion powder
- 1 tsp paprika
- 1 tsp salt
- 1/4 tsp black pepper
- 100 g BBQ sauce

Preparation

1. Mix the garlic powder, onion powder, paprika, salt, and black pepper together.

2. Rub the mixture all over the ribs.

3. Place the ribs in the air fryer basket and cook at 180°C for 25-30 minutes.

4. Brush the BBQ sauce over the ribs and cook for an additional 5 minutes.

Air Fryer Stuffed Mushrooms

Servings: 4

Ingredients

- 8 large mushrooms, stems removed
- 100 g breadcrumbs
- 50 g grated Parmesan cheese
- 1 garlic clove, minced
- 2 tbsp chopped parsley
- 2 tbsp olive oil
- Salt and pepper

Preparation

1. Preheat the air fryer to 200°C.
2. In a small bowl, mix the breadcrumbs, Parmesan cheese, garlic, parsley, and olive oil together.
3. Season the mushroom caps with salt and pepper, and fill each cap with the breadcrumb mixture.
4. Place the stuffed mushrooms in the air fryer basket and cook for 10-12 minutes, until the filling is crispy and golden brown.

Air Fryer Fried Chicken

Servings: 4

Ingredients

- 4 chicken drumsticks
- 200 g buttermilk
- 200 g all-purpose flour
- 1 tsp paprika
- 1 tsp garlic powder
- 1 tsp onion powder
- 1/2 tsp salt
- 1/4 tsp black pepper
- 2 tbsp olive oil

Preparation

1. Soak the chicken drumsticks in buttermilk for at least 30 minutes.

2. In a bowl, mix the flour, paprika, garlic powder, onion powder, salt, and black pepper together.

3. Coat the chicken drumsticks in the flour mixture, shaking off any excess.

4. Brush the chicken drumsticks with olive oil.

5. Place the chicken drumsticks in the air fryer basket and cook at 200°C for 18-20 minutes, flipping halfway through.

Air Fryer Garlic Bread

Servings: 4

Ingredients

- 4 slices of bread
- 50 g butter, melted
- 1 garlic clove, minced
- 1/4 tsp salt
- 1/4 tsp black pepper
- 50 g grated Parmesan cheese

Preparation

1. In a small bowl, mix the melted butter, garlic, salt, black pepper, and Parmesan cheese together.

2. Brush the mixture over the bread slices.

3. Place the bread slices in the air fryer basket and cook at 180°C for 5-7 minutes, until golden brown and crispy.

Air Fryer Cinnamon Sugar Donuts

Servings: 4

Ingredients

- 1 can refrigerated biscuits
- 50 g sugar
- 1 tsp ground cinnamon
- 3 tbsp butter, melted

Preparation

1. Preheat the air fryer to 180°C.

2. Cut each biscuit into quarters.

3. In a small bowl, mix the sugar and cinnamon together.

4. Dip each biscuit quarter in the melted butter, then roll in the cinnamon sugar mixture.

5. Place the biscuit quarters in the air fryer basket and cook for 5-7 minutes, until golden brown and crispy.

Air Fryer Beef Skewers

Servings: 4

Ingredients

- 500g beef sirloin, cut into cubes
- 1 red bell pepper, cut into cubes
- 1 green bell pepper, cut into cubes
- 1 red onion, cut into cubes
- 1 tbsp olive oil
- 1 tsp paprika
- 1 tsp garlic powder
- 1 tsp dried oregano
- 1/2 tsp salt
- 1/4 tsp black pepper

Preparation

1. Soak wooden skewers in water for 30 minutes.

2. Thread the beef, red bell pepper, green bell pepper, and red onion onto the skewers.

3. Brush the skewers with olive oil and sprinkle with paprika, garlic powder, oregano, salt, and black pepper.

4. Place the skewers in the air fryer basket and cook at 200°C for 10-12 minutes, flipping halfway through.

Air Fryer Buffalo Cauliflower

Ingredients

- 1 head cauliflower, cut into florets
- 50 g all-purpose flour
- 1/4 tsp paprika
- 1/4 tsp garlic powder
- 1/4 tsp onion powder
- 1/4 tsp salt
- 1/4 tsp black pepper
- 50 g buffalo sauce
- 2 tbsp butter, melted

Preparation

1. In a small bowl, mix the flour, paprika, garlic powder, onion powder, salt, and black pepper together.

2. Dip the cauliflower florets in the flour mixture, shaking off any excess.

3. Place the cauliflower florets in the air fryer basket and cook at 180°C for 8-10 minutes, shaking the basket halfway through.

4. In a separate bowl, mix the buffalo sauce and melted butter together.

5. Toss the cooked cauliflower in the buffalo sauce mixture, making sure each piece is coated.

Air Fryer Caramelized Bananas

Servings: 4

Ingredients

- 2 ripe bananas, sliced
- 2 tbsp butter, melted
- 2 tbsp brown sugar
- 1 tsp ground cinnamon

Preparation

1. Preheat the air fryer to 200°C.

2. In a small bowl, mix the melted butter, brown sugar, and cinnamon together.

3. Toss the sliced bananas in the mixture.

4. Place the sliced bananas in the air fryer basket and cook for 5-7 minutes, until caramelized.

Air Fryer Bacon

Servings: 4

Ingredients

- 6 slices of bacon

Preparation

1. Preheat the air fryer to 200°C.

2. Place the bacon slices in the air fryer basket, making sure they don't overlap.

3. Cook the bacon for 6-8 minutes, flipping halfway through, until crispy.

Air Fryer Pork Rinds

Servings: 4

Ingredients

- 100 g pork rinds
- 1 tsp smoked paprika
- 1 tsp garlic powder
- 1 tsp onion powder
- 1/2 tsp salt
- 1/4 tsp black pepper

Preparation

1. In a small bowl, mix the smoked paprika, garlic powder, onion powder, salt, and black pepper together.

2. Place the pork rinds in the air fryer basket and cook at 200°C for 4-5 minutes, until crispy.

3. Sprinkle the spice mixture over the cooked pork rinds.

Air Fryer Tofu

Servings: 4

Ingredients

- 350 g firm tofu, cut into cubes
- 50 g cornstarch
- 1/2 tsp garlic powder
- 1/2 tsp onion powder
- 1/4 tsp salt
- 1/4 tsp black pepper
- 1 tbsp olive oil
- 2 tbsp soy sauce

Preparation

1. In a small bowl, mix the cornstarch, garlic powder, onion powder, salt, and black pepper together.

2. Toss the tofu cubes in the cornstarch mixture, shaking off any excess.

3. Place the tofu cubes in the air fryer basket and cook at 200°C for 10-12 minutes, shaking the basket halfway through.

4. In a separate bowl, mix the olive oil and soy sauce together.

5. Toss the cooked tofu in the soy sauce mixture, making sure each piece is coated.

Air Fryer Fried Shrimp

Servings: 4

Ingredients

- 500 g large shrimp, peeled and deveined
- 100 g all-purpose flour
- 2 eggs, beaten
- 200 g panko breadcrumbs
- 1 tsp garlic powder
- 1 tsp paprika
- 1/2 tsp salt
- 1/4 tsp black pepper

Preparation

1. Place the flour, beaten eggs, and panko breadcrumbs mixed with garlic powder, paprika, salt, and black pepper in separate bowls.
2. Dip each shrimp in the flour, then the beaten egg, then the breadcrumb mixture.
3. Place the shrimp in the air fryer basket and cook at 200°C for 5-6 minutes, until crispy and golden brown.

Air Fryer Chimichangas

Servings: 4

Ingredients

- 500 g ground beef
- 100 g salsa
- 1 tsp chili powder
- 1/2 tsp cumin
- 1/2 tsp garlic powder
- 1/2 tsp salt
- 1/4 tsp black pepper
- 8 flour tortillas
- 200 g shredded cheddar cheese

Preparation

1. In a large skillet, cook the ground beef over medium-high heat until browned and cooked through.

2. Stir in the salsa, chili powder, cumin, garlic powder, salt, and black pepper.

3. Lay out a tortilla and place a scoop of the beef mixture in the center.

4. Top the beef mixture with shredded cheese.

5. Fold in the sides of the tortilla and then roll it up like a burrito.

6. Place the chimichangas in the air fryer basket and cook at 200°C for 8-10 minutes, until crispy and golden brown.

Air Fryer Apple Chips

Servings: 4

Ingredients

- 2 apples, cored and thinly sliced
- 1 tbsp cinnamon
- 1 tbsp sugar

Preparation

1. Preheat the air fryer to 120°C.

2. In a small bowl, mix the cinnamon and sugar together.

3. Toss the apple slices in the cinnamon sugar mixture.

4. Place the apple slices in the air fryer basket and cook for 1-2 hours, until crispy and dry.

Air Fryer Pesto Chicken

Servings: 4

Ingredients

- 4 boneless, skinless chicken breasts
- 50 g pesto
- 50 g grated Parmesan cheese
- 1/2 tsp garlic powder
- 1/2 tsp salt
- 1/4 tsp black pepper

Preparation

1. Preheat the air fryer to 200°C.
2. Mix the pesto, Parmesan cheese, garlic powder, salt, and black pepper together in a small bowl.
3. Coat the chicken breasts with the mixture.
4. Place the chicken breasts in the air fryer basket and cook for 12-15 minutes, flipping halfway through, until cooked through and golden brown on the outside.

Printed in Great Britain
by Amazon

37247337R00051